D0815859

Dear Parent:
Your child's love of reading

Every child learns to read in a different way and at his or her own speed. Some go back and forth between reading levels and read favorite books again and again. Others read through each level in order. You can help your young reader improve and become more confident by encouraging his or her own interests and abilities. From books your child reads with you to the first books he or she reads alone, there are I Can Read Books for every stage of reading:

SHARED READING
Basic language, word repetition, and whimsical illustrations, ideal for sharing with your emergent reader

BEGINNING READING
Short sentences, familiar words, and simple concepts for children eager to read on their own

READING WITH HELP
Engaging stories, longer sentences, and language play for developing readers

READING ALONE
Complex plots, challenging vocabulary, and high-interest topics for the independent reader

I Can Read Books have introduced children to the joy of reading since 1957. Featuring award-winning authors and illustrators and a fabulous cast of beloved characters, I Can Read Books set the standard for beginning readers.

A lifetime of discovery begins with the magical words "I Can Read!"

*Visit www.icanread.com for information
on enriching your child's reading experience.*

**Visit www.zonderkidz.com/icanread for more faith-based
I Can Read! titles from Zonderkidz.**

I have set my rainbow in the clouds, and it
will be the sign of the covenant between
me and the earth.
—*Genesis 9:13*

ZONDERKIDZ

Noah's Voyage
Copyright © 2015 by Zondervan
Illustrations © 2015 by David Miles

An **I Can Read Book**

Requests for information should be addressed to:
Zonderkidz, 3900 *Sparks Drive SE, Grand Rapids, Michigan 49546*

Library of Congress Cataloging-in-Publication Data

Noah's voyage / illustrated by David Miles.
    pages   cm. – (Adventure Bible I can read ; Level 2)
    Summary: "With age-appropriate vocabulary and concepts, young readers
learn about Noah and his quest to trust in God and build the ark" – Provided by
publisher.
    Audiences: Ages 4-8.
    ISBN 978-0-310-74683-6 (softcover) – ISBN 0-310-74683-3 (softcover) –
ISBN 978-0-310-74742-0 (epub) – ISBN 978-0-310-74687-4 (epub) –
ISBN 978-0-310-74749-9 (epub)
    1. Noah (Biblical figure)—Juvenile literature. 2. Noah's ark—Juvenile literature.
3. Deluge—Juvenile literature, 4. Bible stories, English—Old Testament—Juvenile
literature. I. Miles, David, 1973- illustrator.
BS580.N6N65   2015
222.1109505—dc23   2014031614

All Scripture quotations, unless otherwise indicated, are taken from The Holy Bible,
New International Version®, *NIV*®. Copyright © 1973, 1978, 1984, 2011 by Biblica, Inc.®
Used by permission. All rights reserved worldwide.

Any internet addresses (websites, blogs, etc.) and telephone numbers in this book are
offered as a resource. They are not intended in any way to be or imply an endorsement
by Zondervan, nor does Zondervan vouch for the content of these sites and numbers
for the life of this book.

No part of this publication may be reproduced, stored in a
retrieval system, or transmitted in any form or by any means—electronic, mechanical,
photocopy, recording, or any other—except for brief quotations in printed reviews,
without the prior permission of the publisher.

Zonderkidz is a trademark of Zondervan.

I Can Read® and I Can Read Book® are trademarks of HarperCollins Publishers.

Editor: Mary Hassinger
Art direction and design: Kris Nelson

Printed in China

20 /DSC / 21 20 19 18 17 16 15 14 13 12 11 10 9 8 7 6 5

It was quiet in Noah's tent.

Everyone was sleeping.

Noah was thinking about his voyage

on the ark.

One day, God came to Noah.

God said, "Noah, you are my friend.

I love you. Please help me."

Noah answered, "Yes, Lord.

I will do whatever you say."

God said, "The people on earth

do not follow my rules.

I am sorry I made man.

But you are a good man, Noah."

"How can I help?" asked Noah.

God said, "There is going to be a flood.

Build an ark. Then two of every creature,

one male and one female, will come.

Put them on the ark. Then wait."

Noah did everything God asked.

Noah's sons Shem, Ham, and Jephath

helped build the ark too.

Noah and his family worked very hard.

God knew he made the right choice.

Noah and his family did the job just right.

God said, "Good work, my friend.

Now all the animals will come.

Put them on the ark. Then you get on too.

The flood will come very soon,"

God said.

So the animals came to Noah.

God sent every kind of living creature.

There were birds, monkeys,
alligators, dogs, bumblebees,
and more …

Some animals went on the top floor.

Some animals went on the middle floor.

Some animals went on the bottom floor.

Then Noah and his family—his wife,

his sons, and their wives—got on the ark.

God closed the window tight.

Noah was 600 years old when

the floodwaters came!

Rain fell on the earth

for forty days and forty nights.

The waters covered everything on earth.

But the water did not cover Noah
and his family.
God kept them safe.

The animals on the ark were safe too.

Noah and his family took care

of the animals.

And they took care of each other.

Even when the rain stopped,
the earth was flooded for 150 days.
God said, "Don't worry, Noah.
You, your family, and the animals
will stay safe."

Noah knew God loved them very much.

He knew they would be safe.

After 150 days, the water started
going down!
After even more days, the ark
came to rest on the tops of
the mountains of Ararat.

Noah opened a window.

He sent a raven to fly

through the air.

"Go! Look for dry land!" said Noah.

Next, Noah sent out a dove to
look for dry land.
But the dove came back.
Noah said, "It is fine, little dove.
We will try again soon."

Seven days later the dove went out

the window again.

When it came back, it had

a fresh olive leaf in its beak.

"You did it, little dove!"

Noah shouted.

When Noah was 601 years old,

the water dried up.

God said, "Come out of the ark, Noah!

Bring your family and the animals!"

All the animals and Noah went out onto
the dry land to live and grow again.

On dry land, Noah built an altar
to honor God.
Noah and his family said thank
you to God for keeping them safe.
Then God did something
wonderful.
He put a rainbow in the sky.
God promised to never flood
the earth ever again.

And Noah knew God
would keep his promise.

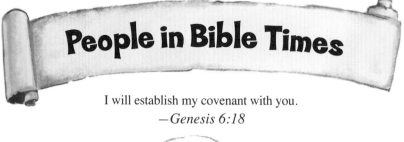

People in Bible Times

I will establish my covenant with you.
—*Genesis 6:18*

Noah

Noah was a good man. When all other men were making God
unhappy, he loved and believed in God. So when God needed help,
he went to Noah and asked him to build the ark. Noah said yes.
Noah trusted God and knew that it was the right thing to do.

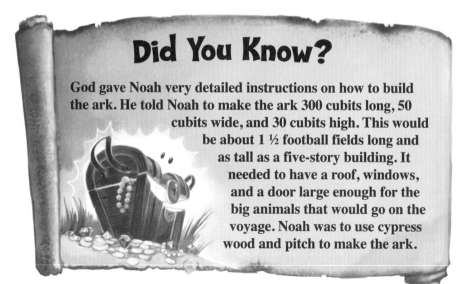

Did You Know?

God gave Noah very detailed instructions on how to build
the ark. He told Noah to make the ark 300 cubits long, 50
cubits wide, and 30 cubits high. This would
be about 1 ½ football fields long and
as tall as a five-story building. It
needed to have a roof, windows,
and a door large enough for the
big animals that would go on the
voyage. Noah was to use cypress
wood and pitch to make the ark.